Africans Came First to Florida

Ponce de Leon brought the first Africans to North America when he landed on Florida's east coast in 1513, more than 100 years prior to the infamous Dutch slave ship that unloaded 20 African captives at Jamestown in 1619. From the beginning, blacks played important roles during Spain's explorations of the New World. When St. Augustine, Florida, was founded by Pedro Menendez de Aviles in 1565, at the site of the Timucua village of Seloy, 50–60 Africans in his crew—both

Where Did Ponce Land?

According to the oldest surviving documents, Ponce de Leon spied the coast of Florida at a latitude of 30º 8', which places his landing at a location just north of St. Augustine. It is a contested claim, but Dr. Sam Turner of the Lighthouse Archaeological Maritime Program (L.A.M.P.) has published several articles that offer significant evidence to support his research that Ponce did indeed make landfall in this area. Other historians have placed the landing at several locations south of St. Augustine, the most popular of these being Melbourne, on Florida's central Atlantic coast.

free and enslaved—would blend their own traditions and customs with the rich cultures of the local Native Americans and other Spanish colonists (the historic site of Seloy has been excavated by numerous archaeologists, most famously Dr. Kathy Deagan, and can be seen today on the property of the Fountain of Youth Archaeological Park in St. Augustine).

Historical documents and baptismal records confirm that within the present-day borders of the continental United States, the child of an enslaved woman was first baptized in St. Augustine in 1595. The first marriage between enslaved Africans was recorded in St. Augustine in 1598, along with the first recorded birth of a child born to an enslaved couple, in 1606.

The founding of St. Augustine by Pedro Menéndez de Avilés and his conquistadors

A Spanish Safe Haven in Florida

J UST as in the West Indies, vast profits from agriculture were earned from the abusive industry of capturing, enslaving, and brutally controlling the labor of African and African-American people. Slave traders from England, Spain, France, Portugal, Denmark, and the Netherlands operated from the west coast of Africa to the Caribbean Islands and South, Central, and North American colonies, with only pirates and privateers to fear. The control of land in the Americas easily became the spark of international war. As a result, European land disputes in the southern colonies of North America would increase as English colonies expanded and prospered in territories once claimed by Spain. Enslaved blacks would be caught in the middle.

When the English colony of Carolina was established in 1670, serious issues arose over the question of where Carolina began and Spanish Florida ended. Broadside advertisements appeared in London as early as 1668, recruiting settlers to reap their fortunes from free land on the "Florida-Coast." Carolina's original charter was drawn up by the English Parliament to include territory as far south as Cape Canaveral, Florida. But Spain was no beginner in this process of grabbing land and pressed their claims of Spanish rights for lands as far north as Port Royal in present-day South Carolina. Considering that as early as 1570 Spanish missions had once occupied a site on the Virginia shores of the Chesapeake Bay, claiming lands that pushed Spanish borders into South Carolina was not inconceivable. But an English colony in Carolina, with a major port springing up in Charles Town, added new threats of piracy for the annual silver fleet sailing the Gulf Stream for Spain, as well as raids on St. Augustine.

CAROLINA

Originally, North and South Carolina were one very large colony, with land claims stretching as far south as Cape Canaveral in Spanish Florida. In 1670, England's King Charles II officially granted colonial status to the region and gave the political and economic control of the colony to a group of investors known as the Lords Proprietors. They patterned their manner for making Carolina financially successful after the plantation-driven economy of the island of Barbados. In 1710, after years of political in-fighting between the land owners of the northern and southern regions of Carolina, the colony was divided into North Carolina and South Carolina. Neither officially received Crown Colony status until 1729.

DISPUTED LANDS OF CAROLINA AND FLORIDA

CAROLINA

By

H. Moll *Geographer*

The English *Claim the Property of Carolina from Lat. 29 &c. Degrees as part of Cabot's Discoveries who set out from Bristol in 1498, at the Charge of King Henry ÿ 7th but they did not take Possession of that Country till King Charles the II's time in 1663 who Granted a Patent to divers Persons to plant all the Territories within the North Lat. of 31 to 36 Deg. and so West in a direct line to the South Sea.*

In 1693, King Carlos II of Spain fueled the land dispute further with a royal edict declaring that any enslaved person who fled to Florida from the English colonies would be legally free. In order to maintain their freedom after arriving in Florida, former slaves were required to take an oath of loyalty to the Spanish Crown, serve in the local militia, and convert to Catholicism. Many historians believe this represents the beginning of the Underground Railroad; only in this case, slaves were fleeing south to find their freedom rather than north.

However, this doesn't mean that the Spanish were acting purely out of compassion for enslaved people, as no Spanish-held slaves were offered this same opportunity. Spain's primary goal was to bankrupt the Carolina colony and ruin English plantation owners and investors. Fewer slaves meant fewer cash crops that could be planted, harvested, and shipped back to England. Spain's offer of refuge would also cost English slave owners a great deal of money as they attempted to either retrieve runaway slaves or replace them. In addition, by extending this hope of freedom to the enslaved population of Carolina, Spain would be boosting its own numbers in Florida, both in fighting men and workers of all ages and

England, Great Britain, *the* United Kingdom
WHICH ONE IS IT?

THIS is one of the more confusing topics about Britain for Americans to digest. Some think that these three titles are basically disjointed references for the same place. Others would guess that they are nicknames, in the same manner that the United States is referred to as "America," "the U.S." or "the States." But it's a wee more complicated than that. England was an independent kingdom that united with (some might say absorbed) Wales in 1536. The region would be governed under the name and crown of England, with the capital at London. Scotland became the third member of the union in 1707, creating what became known as Great Britain. The island of Ireland was added in 1801, and the official name changed once again to the United Kingdom. But the southern districts of Ireland— 5/6ths of the island—waged bloody civil war for the next 121 years, winning their independence in 1922. This left only 1/6 of the island, now known as Northern Ireland, under British rule. However, the entire archipelago of islands, including a free and independent Ireland, is still known as the British Isles...where not everyone is British and all continue to be known by their ancestral birthrights as English, Welsh, Scots, and Irish...except the folks from Northern Ireland who are British...but are still Irish. Now, was that so hard?

THE BRITISH ISLES

genders. More families in the colony meant more stability.

This colonial "no man's land" of overlapping territories between Carolina and Florida quickly became a lightning rod for future conflicts. Great Britain eventually carved out the colony of Georgia from this region in 1733 to create a buffer zone between St. Augustine and Charles Town. Spain countered this move in 1738 by authorizing Governor Manuel de Montiano to establish Fort Mose, the first free-black community in what is now the United States, just two miles north of St. Augustine. In 1740, Fort Mose would become a rallying point during an invasion by British General James Oglethorpe. After evacuating to St. Augustine, the Spanish army and Fort Mose's black militia—led by Francisco Menendez, himself a former British slave—drove the British from their land in a resounding victory. But by 1763, trouble was brewing in the distance, and once again it was the black population that would be caught in the middle.

FORT MOSE

From 1986-1988, archaeologist Kathy Deagan and her team from the University of Florida successfully located the remains of Gracia Real de Santa Teresa de Mose—Fort Mose. Missing from the landscape, as well as American history books, for 170 years, Dr. Deagan returned to the surface many historical artifacts, as well as a new understanding of the first free-black community in the present-day United States. New directives for research were now available to Dr. Jane Landers, Project Historian on the dig, making it possible to take this new information and weave a more complete history of Fort Mose and the individuals who lived there as free Spanish subjects during the years 1738-1740, and then at the re-built Fort Mose from 1752-1763.

THE UNDERGROUND RAILROAD

For years historians have traced the movements of runaway slaves from the United States into Canada from the late 18th century through to the Civil War. Abolitionists (those who wanted to abolish slavery) referred to homes, barns, stores, etc., where it was known that these refugees could find safe shelter as "stations," and those who risked their lives organizing these operations as "conductors."

However, from 1693-1763, thousands of English/British slaves fled southward from the Carolinas and Georgia to the officially sanctioned haven of Florida. Many historians now believe that these people forged the beginnings of the Underground Railroad. Unfortunately, slaves running to Spanish Florida during this time did not have the added support of "conductors" or "stations."

LET THERE BE GEORGIA!

Once England established the colony of Carolina on the Atlantic coast of North America, colonial hostilities between London and Madrid increased rapidly. As Carolina prospered and the rich port at Charles Town grew in importance, threats from Spanish Florida grew increasingly worrisome to English investors. In 1733, Great Britain laid final claim to the disputed lands that would be called Georgia, after King George II. The idea was to stabilize the region between St. Augustine and Charles Town with British towns, British subjects, and British troops. Savannah was established when General James Oglethorpe and 120 settlers sailed up the Savannah River and selected the protected bluffs for their new colonial capital. Destined to become a mini-Charles Town, Savannah grew quickly as Oglethorpe made a lasting peace with Yamacraw chief Tomochichi. Initially, rum, lawyers, and slavery were illegal.

1763: Drastic Change for Blacks in the Southern Colonies

In 1762, Spain gambled (poorly) by jumping into the French and Indian War at the last minute in an attempt to reap cheap profits from the outcome. In doing so, they sacrificed the hope of freedom for thousands of British-held slaves in the southern colonies—particularly those in Georgia and South Carolina who were close enough to Florida to make an attempted escape feasible. After the 1763 Treaty of Paris, the safe haven of Spanish Florida was now under British rule.

Britain believed that the new colony was too vast to govern effectively. Parliament chose to divide Florida into two separate colonies, keeping St. Augustine as the capital of East Florida, while Pensacola would be the new capital of West Florida. East Florida looked very much like the present-day peninsula of Florida, with its western border at the Apalachicola River. West Florida's northern boundary was established at the 31st parallel and would include the panhandle of present-day Florida, the lower halves of Alabama and Mississippi, and all of Louisiana east of the Mississippi River (see map on Page 11). In 1764, Parliament expanded West Florida's northern boundary from the 31st parallel to 32° 28', enlarging the colony by more than double. Only the new British colony of Quebec was larger geographically.

Havana for Florida

In 1762, at the very end of the Seven Years War (known in North America as the French and Indian War), the British captured Havana—Spain's most critical port in the Caribbean. In order to get Havana back, the Spanish handed over all of Florida, which stretched from the Mississippi Valley to the Atlantic Ocean. Britain would divide the vast region into the two separate colonies of East Florida and West Florida, with capitals at St. Augustine and Pensacola. Britain also forced France to leave New Orleans, but curiously allowed Spain to take possession of the city and control the lower portion of the Mississippi delta. In 1764, Britain raised the northern boundary of West Florida another 78.2 miles, from the 31st parallel to 32º 8'.

In East Florida, just the lands east of the St. Johns River were considered suitable for settlement. Blacks continued to pour into the region, but no longer as freed people. Once British plantations

THE BRITISH AMERICAS

Hudson's

R. Missouri

L. Superior

Quebec

R. St. Lawrence

Montreal

Champlain

Acadia

C. Breton

Louisbourg

L. Michigan

L. Huron

Oswego

New England

Crown Point

F. Niagara

L. Ontario

Ticonderoga

Boston

Nova Scotia

L. Erie

Fort Duquesne

Pennsylvania

New York

Philadelphia

R. Ohio

Alleghany Mts

Virginia

Chesapeake Bay

R. Mississippi

Georgia

Bermudas

Rio Grande

R. del Norte

New Orleans

W. Florida

E. Florida

GULF OF MEXICO

C. Sable

Bahama Is.

Tropic of Cancer

ATLANTIC

Campeachy Bay

Mexico

Cuba

Porto Rico

St. Eustat.

Santiago

Nevis

An.

G. of Honduras

Jamaica

Hayti I.

St. Christopher

Guadeloupe

D.

Martinique

CARIBBEAN SEA

St. Vincent

Grenada

Cartagena

Porto Bello

R. Orinoco

SOUTH AMERICA

EASTERN & CENTRAL AMERICA
1763

British
French
Spanish
Dutch

English Miles

10

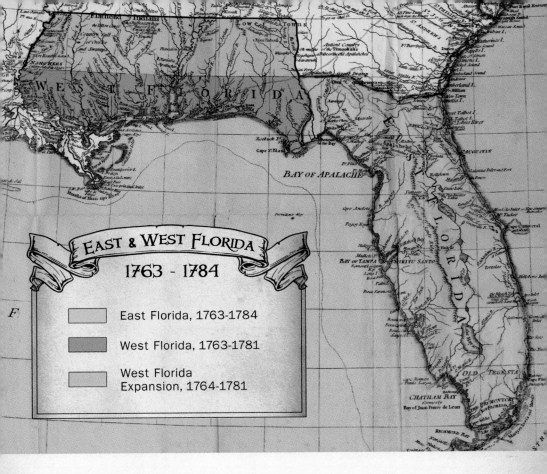

East & West Florida
1763 - 1784

- East Florida, 1763-1784
- West Florida, 1763-1781
- West Florida Expansion, 1764-1781

began to dot the East and West Florida landscapes, the number of black slaves would dominate the population totals. The world of hope that many came to depend upon had disappeared.

By the time of the American Revolution there were very few changes in the hostile relationship between the empires of Great Britain and Spain. In this era of European history, winning wars meant gaining colonies. It didn't matter what the wars were about as long as they were fighting over something—and usually it was the result of either French interference or French encouragement. France had been kicked out of North America after the French and Indian War and wanted revenge. Great Britain, on the other hand had drastically increased its colonial holdings in the Americas by adding Grenada in the southern Caribbean, and in North America—in addition to the other 13 colonies you may have heard about—they now claimed East Florida, West Florida, Quebec, and Nova Scotia. The British Americas now held 33 colonies, stretching from Nova Scotia in the north to Grenada at the southernmost tip of the Caribbean Sea. At the geographic center lay East Florida and West Florida, with St. Augustine possessing the only pair of masonry fortresses south of the Chesapeake Bay.

While European attitudes toward one another changed very little, there were tremendous changes in the relationship between Great Britain and its high-strung American colonies. As tensions rose between colonists and the mother country, the lives of blacks within these colonies became even more uncertain than they already were. Imagine how bizarre it must have seemed to enslaved blacks during the Stamp Act Crisis of 1765, as they watched mobs of slave-holding Sons of Liberty march through the streets of cities like Charles Town and Savannah shouting for the "shackles and chains of tyranny" to be removed. There were many other contradictions, one being that American slave owners refused to participate in the British tradition of arming slaves in times of crisis. When colonists were embattled

Who *Names*
THESE WARS?

WAS it the French and Indian War or the Seven Years War...or both? Were they even the same war? In truth, this conflict is best described as the first "world war" in history. Fighting began on March 28, 1754, when British militia, led by a 21-year old Lt. Colonel George Washington, fired on an encampment of 35 French soldiers. Fighting would rage in North America for the next 9 years, but it didn't become a full-blown war across the globe until 1756 (1756-1763...seven years!). On one side, this war involved Britain, Prussia, Portugal, the Iroquois Confederacy, and the German states of Brunswick, Hanover, Hesse-Kassal, and Schaumburg. On the other side were France, Spain, Austria, Russia, Sweden, Saxony, eight allied Native American nations, and the Mughal Empire in India. Fighting spread from North America to Europe, South America, Africa, India, the Philippines, and on every known ocean of that day. It would be interesting to look up how many other names this same war took on in other regions of the world!

If they were to give an award for the craziest name for a war, the hands-down winner would be the War of Jenkins Ear. At the conclusion of the War of Spanish Succession (also known as Queen Anne's War, 1700-1713), Spain granted Britain certain trade agreements with their "New World" colonies. By 1729, British merchants felt that the arrangements had become increasingly unreliable and unstable. By 1739, these trade issues erupted into yet another war. Surprisingly, the British felt the need for a better excuse for war than the pettiness of merchants (though that excuse was often employed). They needed an example of damaged national honor, and they found it in an incident that occurred in 1731—eight years earlier! A British ship's captain named Robert Jenkins had his ear sliced off by the Spanish when Jenkins's ship was searched for smuggled goods. Huzzah! The British now had "good reason" to incite the masses to take up arms, which in turn gave us the most ridiculous name for a war in history.

THE STAMP ACT OF 1765

Many scholars believe that the Stamp Act Crisis of 1765 was the actual beginning of the American Revolution. Britain hoped to tax the American colonies on imports for such basic items as legal documents, playing cards, newspapers, and diplomas. John Adams declared that "The people, even to the lowest ranks, have become more attentive to their liberties, more inquisitive about them, and more determined to defend them, than they were ever before known." Though it would be another 10 years before fighting broke out, a spirit of rebellion had been born.

with Native Americans or haunted by local bandits—even when Britain was at war with other empires—most slaves in North America had few options but to hope they would be protected by their owners. Otherwise, their only options would be to hide or to defend themselves with field tools.

For American slave owners, it wasn't simply a fear that once the crisis was over these armed slaves would then revolt. The issues were more deeply rooted in the social structure of the American colonies, especially on the southern plantations. American culture had become saturated over the years with endless efforts to deny blacks any sense of dignity. One way of doing this was to forbid enslaved men from carrying firearms in times of trouble. This denied them the time-honored right of defending themselves and those they loved. This would explain why George Washington, a slave holder, initially refused to allow blacks into the ranks of the Continental Army.

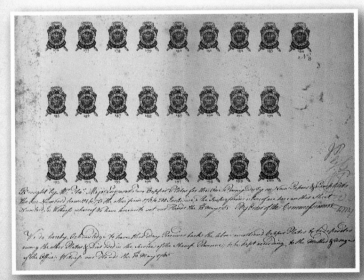

Proof sheet of one-penny stamps submitted for approval to Commissioners of Stamps by engraver, May 10, 1765. **Does it say what these stamps were to be used for?**

British Proclamations of "Freedom"

ONCE shots split the air at Lexington and Concord on April 19, 1775, the rebellion took a great leap toward becoming a revolution. The British were quick to remember how Spain had used the longing for freedom among British slaves to attack the Carolina

JOHN MURRAY, 4TH EARL OF DUNMORE

They Seem Like the Same Thing!

Rebellion, revolution; sedition, treason—they seem like the same thing, but they're really very different. When disagreements between colonists and their mother country took some form of action, such as the mob violence by the Sons of Liberty in Boston or the fighting at Lexington and Concord, it was called a rebellion. Even after the full-scale battle of Bunker Hill (Breed's Hill), King George III read to Parliament a "Proclamation of Rebellion" against the American colonies. It would not become a revolution until the Continental Congress declared that full and complete independence was their goal. The difference between sedition and treason seems just as confusing, but sedition was to openly promote rebellion, while treason was to take action in the revolution that followed.

economy. Now Britain would have the opportunity to use that same hunger within the colonial slave population to wreck the rebellion.

In 1775, the governor of Virginia, John Murray, 4th Earl of Dunmore, offered freedom to any slave in his colony willing to escape their chains and fight on the side of the Crown. This has been known ever since as Dunmore's Proclamation. Lord Dunmore named this new fighting force the Ethiopian Regiment and provided quality weapons and new uniforms to instill pride, honor, and encouragement for their actions. But Dunmore's attitude toward runaway slaves was not an official policy and would be interpreted in many different ways by British officers and officials.

Loyalist or Patriot?

The labels of "Loyalist" and "Patriot" are two of the more curious terms of the American Revolution. In the American Continental Congress, a Loyalist was a scoundrel who still bowed down to a tyrant, King George III. A patriot, on the other hand, was a believer in the fight for independence—patriotic to the "Glorious Cause." However, on the streets of London (and New York City, for that matter), a true patriot was an individual who was loyal to king and country—in other words, a Loyalist. So, if you were speaking with a "king's man," a Loyalist and a Patriot were the same thing. However, anyone in rebellion was...a rebel!

Such was the case in East Florida. As each southern colony fell to the rebellion in the summer and early fall of 1775, Loyalists and their slaves began an exodus south to the Floridas. East Florida would be the only colony south of the Canadian border to never lower the Union Jack throughout the course of the American Revolution. Lord Dunmore sent many freed slaves to East Florida in 1776, on the same ships as prisoners-of-war and evacuated Loyalists. Soon the number of blacks in East Florida—free and enslaved—was growing fast enough to concern the governor, Lt. Colonel Patrick Tonyn. Governor Tonyn wrote to Lord George Germain, Secretary of State of the American Colonies, that in order to frustrate more invasion attempts by the American rebels, he "established and armed the Companies of malitia (sic), who may be employed in case of invasion, and will be at all times useful in keeping in awe the Negroes who multiply amazingly." In Tonyn's mind, the concern was fundamental: more and more Loyalist refugees were coming to East Florida as the southern colonies fell in domino-fashion to the rebellion. Blacks, both those freed by Dunmore's Proclamation as well as the slaves of southern Loyalist refugees, were quickly outnumbering the white population in East Florida. Governor Tonyn, a slave owner himself, believed the situation was a potential powder keg and

Rebellion in the Southern Colonies

Once fighting broke out on April 19, 1775, it didn't take long for the rebellion to sweep the southern colonies. North Carolina fell in late May and Virginia in June, 1775. Georgia deposed their royal governor in June, also, but allowed him to remain in office as an advisor until they finally put him under house arrest for being obnoxious. South Carolina fell two months later, in September. By early fall 1775, the only southern colonies that remained loyal to the Crown were East Florida and West Florida. Unlike the other colonies where some of the people were Loyalists, some Rebels, and some neutral, British subjects in the two Florida colonies were adamantly loyal to King George III.

There were more than two sides in this war

The American Revolution wasn't as simple as Redcoats against Bluecoats, or Loyalists versus Rebels. John Adams wrote that the population was divided into thirds: those in rebellion, those loyal to the Crown, and those who simply wanted to be left alone. Helpless civilians trying to keep their families and farms safe often supported whichever army was marching down the road. And don't forget that

Native Americans were greatly affected by the outcome of the Revolution, as well, and fought for whichever side offered them the greatest opportunity for a lasting peace. Most often they chose to either fight for the British or take no stance at all. Native Americans understood that if the "Virginians" won their war of independence, a Native American war of independence would just be beginning.

proposed to treat all blacks with suspicion until given a reason to believe otherwise. In 1779, General Sir Henry Clinton, the commander-in-chief of all British troops in the American colonies (1778–1782), declared what would be known as the Philipsburg Proclamation. The difference between the Philipsburg Proclamation and Lord Dunmore's decree was that General Clinton offered freedom to any enslaved person who escaped to British camps—man, woman, or child.

These actions played a tremendous role in damaging any hope of reconciliation between the Crown and its colonists. Not only were American planters who had already set their minds toward independence affected, but political fence-straddlers became outraged as well. Even Loyalist plantation owners felt the strain as their slaves also ran toward British camps in hopes that their proper identities wouldn't be discovered. Officers trying to accurately identify slaves that they didn't know personally had a difficult task. Slaves represented large investments, and losses due to mistakes in identification by British officers could potentially drive

GEN. SIR HENRY CLINTON

some to financial ruin. It would take careful examination of scars from beatings and body types—sometimes under near-battlefield conditions—by military personnel who might well have an army bearing down on them. To many officers in the field, a runaway slave represented a much needed pair of hands digging trenches, shoring up breastworks, or in some cases manning another musket on the line. When under a bayonet charge from an opposing army, even

BREASTWORKS

THROUGHOUT the 18th and 19th centuries, American armies typically rejected the European tradition of the "slaughter line" style of fighting, choosing rather to fortify their surroundings in the field whenever possible (European armies would employ this tactic at times, but many field commanders felt it was not an honorable way to fight a war). If a fence line or walled field was available, all the better, but often soldiers had to hastily build breastworks. Breastworks were typically barriers of wood or stones (Andrew Jackson used cotton bales at the Battle of New Orleans) with as much earth as could be dug piled on top and around to provide protection against cannonballs. Breastworks also gave fighting men a safe cover while reloading their muskets. The earth used to solidify the breastworks was likely taken from a trench dug in front of the breastworks so that the defenses were made higher simply by making the ground in front of them lower. It wasn't uncommon for British commanders to use former slaves seeking freedom to perform the backbreaking work of digging and building breastworks.

Rampart: interior slope
Bombproofs: earth-covered rooms for shelter
Parapet: breastworks protective "walls"
Abatis: fallen trees or pikes to slow a charging army

Parapet · Rampart · Bombproof · Abatis

the landed nobility rarely challenged the color of the man's skin standing beside him in battle.

But upon arrival in British camps, runaway slaves learned quickly that stepping up to fight didn't guarantee them their freedom. One outrageous series of atrocities began in June 1779, when 2,500 British troops under General Augustine Prevost retreated from a hastily crafted, but well-meaning assault on Charles Town. Back in February, Prevost's second-in-command, Lt. Colonel Archibald Campbell, had been forced to make a hurried retreat from Augusta to the safety of Savannah. A much larger American army from South Carolina under General Benjamin Lincoln was advancing quickly on Campbell's position and was sure to overtake him. Prevost's only hope to protect Campbell was to attack the abandoned Charles Town. Once the maneuver was realized, Lincoln had no choice but to redirect his army back to Charles Town. It took Lincoln three days to catch up to Prevost, giving Campbell time to reach Savannah safely.

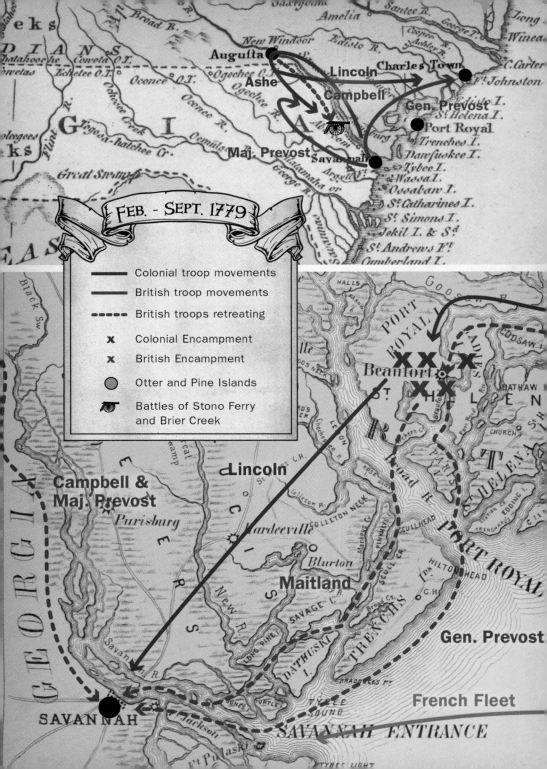

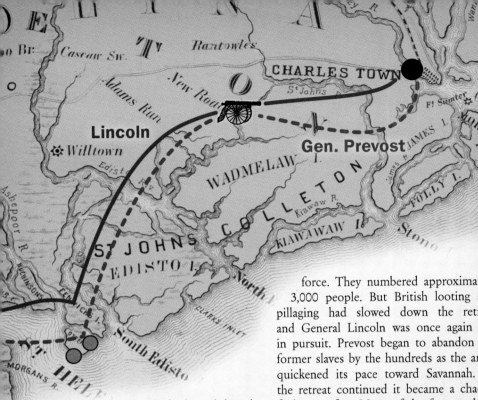

Prevost then began a difficult withdrawal back to Savannah by island-hopping down the Carolina/Georgia coast line along the northern regions of the Gullah-Geechee Corridor—an intracoastal "end around," if you will. During the retreat, Prevost's army plundered the countryside as they went. Livestock, furniture, clothing, crops— valuables of every kind—were targeted by raiding parties. Enslaved human beings were treated little better than pack animals as they were viewed as "property" that not only could walk rather than take up room in a cart, but could also carry other plundered loot and perform hard labor on military work details.

Accounts of this march have varied slightly over the years as new information has been recovered, but we know that a large number of slaves ran to this army for safety, while a great many others were taken by force. They numbered approximately 3,000 people. But British looting and pillaging had slowed down the retreat and General Lincoln was once again hot in pursuit. Prevost began to abandon the former slaves by the hundreds as the army quickened its pace toward Savannah. As the retreat continued it became a chaotic flight to safety. Many of the former slaves on this march were wounded or too sick to travel. Some 400 people were forced to stay behind when the British left Pine Island. A large number of the abandoned slaves swam or floated to Otter Island, where several of them died from disease and exposure. Many of the former slaves tried to latch themselves to evacuation vessels sent to rescue Prevost's army, but soldiers hacked at their bindings with bayonets. Many drowned. It's reported that those who survived Prevost's march to Savannah were ultimately shipped to the West Indies and sold back into slavery.

There were other examples in East Florida of black Loyalists, both free and enslaved, who came to St. Augustine during the war, received temporary protection by the British when work was needed on the defenses of the colony, then shipped into the West Indies for sale.

The
GULLAH-GEECHEE
Corridor

THE Gullah-Geechee Corridor is home to unique African and African-American culture and customs unlike those anywhere else. The corridor stretches roughly from Hampstead, NC, down the Sea Islands and coastal tidewater lands, to the Matanzas Inlet south of St. Augustine, FL. Though rice and cotton plantations dominated the corridor throughout the 1700s, geography, disease, and climate kept the region isolated from outside influences. In this unusual setting, Gullah and Geechee people preserved strong elements of their ancestors' African heritage, such as religion, language, art, and food. Gullah and Geechee people have remained relatively remote even into the 21st century. Gullah and Geechee communities have worked to preserve their way of life, while facing the challenges of coastal development and tourism that have displaced many of their communities and threatened the existence of others.

FOR THOSE
WHO FOUND FREEDOM…?

CERTAINLY, there were instances of former slaves who made their way to East Florida and found that tiny sliver of hope they were looking for. But the primary concern of British authorities in St. Augustine was not liberating slaves or proclamations of freedom—it was the defense of the colony against American and Spanish invasion. As early as 1775, slaves worked on the military fortifications of St. Augustine by upgrading the defenses of the 17th-century masonry fortresses, particularly the Castillo de San Marcos. They also repaired old defensive lines outside the city gates, built new earthworks on the city's western and southern perimeters and redoubts along the St. Johns River, and constructed Fort Tonyn on the St. Marys River.

After the Spanish captured Pensacola in May 1781, Lt. Colonel Lewis V. Fuser requisitioned over nine-hundred slaves from the plantations of East Florida in order to prepare the western earthwork defenses of St. Augustine for the anticipated invasion of Bernardo de Galvez from West Florida. Initially, Fuser utilized ten percent of the colony's slave population for this work; a

The Castillo de San Marcos

EARTHWORKS

Earthworks were exactly what they sound like—breastworks without solid materials, such as stone or wood (or cotton bales) to give the freshly dug soil something solid to pack around. Earthworks were often built for the simple reason that the solid materials needed were unavailable. While breastworks were preferred over earthworks, an army had to work with what they had, and often with an opposing army just over the ridge. Before the land-fill projects of the 1880s, St. Augustine was located on a peninsula. The swamp on the city's western border created enough of a defensive barrier of its own that earthworks were all that was needed to secure this area. But just to be on the safe side, Spanish Bayonet (Yucca) plants were planted on the crest of the earthworks. You can still see the remains of these earthworks today!

number that would eventually rise to 20 percent. This wasn't unusual. Slaves were used by the British to build the defenses of Savannah and Charles Town, as well. Due to the timeframes of each siege on those cities and the multiple evacuations of Loyalists and their slaves to St. Augustine throughout the war, it's not unthinkable that many of these slaves may have worked on the defenses of all three colonial capitals.

But there was a sick method to the madness of how the British treated those who came to them with nothing more than a hope that their dreams of freedom would be honored. By putting such a large labor force to work on the colony's defenses, Governor Tonyn was also following Sir Henry Clinton's official policy for containing slave revolts. It was Clinton's intention to put the strongest, healthiest slaves who responded to the Philipsburg Proclamation to work either on Loyalist plantations to keep production and profits up, or in other support roles for the army, such as "sappers," grave diggers, stretcher bearers, and to construct breastworks and fortifications. The idea was to prevent

Remains of St. Augustine's British earthworks on Cordova Ave., near Orange Street

WHAT IN THE WORLD IS A SAPPER?

It's not uncommon to see the word "sapper" used by Revolutionary War historians—it was used in this booklet! But the word "sapper" is a classic example of an accepted historical term being used incorrectly, even at the highest levels of education. "Sapper" is actually a 19th-century term that has been conveniently ushered backward into 18th-century definitions. Taken from the ancient-French word *sapeur*, sappers were soldiers who performed the very difficult tasks of digging trenches, building breastworks, and cutting trees through thick forests to make roads. But during the American Revolution these jobs were quite often done by slaves who had run to the British lines to fight against their former owners. During the 18th century, the official title for these men was "pioneer"—a term quite appropriate in this era for those who, in addition to other duties, were literally blazing trails and cutting roads through the wilderness. So...Daniel Boone the *sapper*? That just doesn't sound right!!

slave revolts by intentionally exhausting and improperly feeding those believed to be physically capable of breaking out of their deplorable work conditions and leading others to revolt.

Like the American slave owners who demanded to be free of the chains of tyranny, the British proclamations of freedom were also filled with contradictions and hypocrisy. Enslaved people served the European empires best as pawns rather than human beings. Lord Dunmore, for example, armed the slaves of Virginia for the defense of the colony; however, though Dunmore developed the concept, it was the slaves themselves who

Road cleared by pioneers.

"Taking" a COLONY

WHEN we discuss the American army "taking" a colony, it doesn't necessarily mean that the entire geographic region of the colony was under the control of American armies and ruled by American political leaders. As we *tell* the story today, to take a colony typically means that the capital had been captured. But, as the story was *lived* during the Revolution, by no means does that suggest that peace was restored to the entire colony. For example, when Williamsburg, the capital of Virginia, was taken by armed rebel militia in June 1775, Virginia was proclaimed to be an independent state. But there were still many people in Virginia who were Loyalists and the deposed royal governor, Lord Dunmore, went to great lengths to raise armies to bring down the new American government. The capitals of South Carolina and Georgia were both taken three different times: first to the rebels in the summer of 1775, then to the British in 1778 (Savannah) and 1780 (Charleston), then a third time when the victorious American armies returned in 1782, at the end of the war. But even though the capitals of these two colonies were occupied and under the control of one side or the other, the backcountry regions of the Carolinas and Georgia were constantly in flames and the fighting never ended, as neither side could maintain control for any length of time. Peace only came when the British abandoned all hope of victory in 1782, and those loyal to the Crown were evacuated to East Florida.

Fighting in the southern backcountry was vicious and put entire families in harm's way.

first put the plan into motion. Dunmore informed Lord Dartmouth in a letter dated May 1, 1775 of his thoughts on this idea of forming an army out of runaway slaves, but he didn't officially enact his proclamation until six months later, on November 7. Just days after Dunmore wrote to Dartmouth, General Thomas Gage, the commander-in-chief of British troops throughout North America (1774–1775), got wind of Dunmore's idea and put the plan into effect immediately.

But the slaves of Virginia didn't need *permission* to run to freedom and didn't wait for British protocol. As soon as additional British troops arrived in the Chesapeake Bay from St. Augustine to shore up the strength of Dunmore's forces, slaves from the area bolted for British camps and volunteered to fight in return for their freedom. Meanwhile, on the York River, Captains John McCartney and Matthew Squire of the *Mercury* and the *Otter*, respectively, welcomed runaway

GEN. THOMAS GAGE

slaves aboard their ships and provided them with employment. Later, on October 15, the British Prime Minister, Lord North, informed King George III of the dire circumstances awaiting the rebels of Virginia and South Carolina should the larger number of black slaves in these two colonies rise up in revolt. With slaves already putting Dunmore's idea into action, ships' captains eagerly taking on this new-found source of labor, and political approval coming from the highest level, it should make us wonder why Lord Dunmore waited until November 7th to enact his proclamation. The truth of the matter was that Dunmore wasn't concerned with freeing slaves nearly as much as he was hoping to hold the rebellion at arm's length for as long as possible. Dunmore believed that the threat of slave revolt was much more frightening, and therefore more effective, than the act itself.

"Follow me, boys!"

In the Service of the Crown

BLACKS did much more than run away to dig ditches or pilot small ships—they also fought. Slaves and freedmen alike could be found in the militia, special companies of rangers, and even in provincial army regiments. In East Florida, freedmen and slaves made up 15% of the regular army and militia units, and they were used to protect the St. Marys River frontier from invasion from Georgia. Lt. Colonel Thomas Brown, the great-grandson of Sir Isaac Newton, welcomed blacks into his command with the East Florida Rangers. The Rangers were basically Governor Tonyn's hand-picked, personal army—a "black ops" unit, if you will—and Brown became the

stuff of legends. Thomas Brown believed that the best way to keep slaves from revolt and former slaves loyal was to give them weapons and treat them like men. This would bode well for the Rangers on many occasions, on many battlefields.

Governor Tonyn strongly advocated to the East Florida Council that the slaveholders of East Florida must report to military authorities the number of their slaves who could be trusted with firearms. Following Lord Dunmore's precedent when he established the Ethiopian Brigade, four companies of enlisted black soldiers were formed in St. Augustine on August 20, 1776. It wasn't that Governor Tonyn now trusted the large black population in

Thomas Brown
and the East Florida Rangers

Thomas Brown was just 25 years old when he was attacked by not less than fifty Sons of Liberty. He was beaten near to death, scalped multiple times, tarred and feathered, and lost at least two toes after hot irons were put to his feet. He would recover to become one of the most feared Loyalists in the southern colonies. Governor Tonyn gave him the rank of Lt. Colonel and the command of a rugged group of backcountry woodsmen and allied Creek warriors known as the East Florida Rangers. They made lightning-strike raids, rustled cattle, and

provided invaluable intelligence to the British military through a network of spies they set up in every city, town, and village in the Carolinas and Georgia. General Prevost would ultimately absorb Brown's Rangers into the British regular army, renaming them the King's Rangers. They were with Prevost throughout his campaigns into Georgia and they held their position with honor during the British victory at Savannah in 1779, when Prevost's 3,000 troops were outnumbered by 10,000 French and American regulars and militia.

"They're coming from every direction!"

East Florida—he trusted the discipline of the British army. It was within this rigid structure that Colonel Charles Tonyn, the governor's father, had raised him, and the same system under which Tonyn himself spent 33 years of his life. To ensure that rigid military discipline would be enforced, all of the officers and non-commissioned officers in the new black companies were seasoned British regulars.

Carrying weapons wasn't the only difference between black soldiers in the American army and the British army. When a former slave was allowed to enlist in a black unit of the British army, such as Sir Henry Clinton's Black Pioneers and Guides, he was required to recite the following oath: "I, [name], do swear that I enter freely and voluntarily into His Majesty's service and I do enlist myself without the least compulsion or persuasion into the Negro Company...."

Who can know the impact of phrases like "freely and voluntarily," or "enlist *myself*" on former slaves as they were ushered back into the human race by offering a pledge of loyalty in a simple ceremony. Not since

Discipline under fire

Olaudah Equiano, 1745-1797

OLAUDAH Equiano was just eleven years old when he was captured in Africa by Dutch slave traders in 1756. After surviving the murderous voyage across the Atlantic Ocean, the young boy was purchased in Virginia by Michael Henry Pascal, a lieutenant in the British navy. Equiano served in the Royal Navy as Pascal's attendant until he was nineteen. Now an able seaman, he was sold in 1763 to a Philadelphia Quaker who put the young man's nautical skills to work in the business of international trade. In 1766, Equiano had earned enough money to purchase his own freedom and move to England to gain an education. His quest for adventure would take him back to the sea, where in 1773 he embarked on an expedition toward the North Pole in search of the fabled Northwest Passage. His autobiography, which tells in stark detail an 11-year old boy's view of a slave ship, plus many other adventures at sea, is considered to be one of the greatest known works of its day on the strength of spirit that drove this man to overcome the horrors of slavery.

1789 manuscript of Olaudah Equiano's autobiography

these men first laid eyes on white slavers had they realized such entitlements as free choice or voluntary actions. Given that the traditional relationship between slaves and their British owners could only be described as horrifying, the call to freedom was powerful enough that blacks could defend a British colony regardless of this history. And there were other motives as well. The consequences of being captured—whether in battle or simply on the run—were severe enough that the best choice for most was to fight, and fight fiercely. It was also an opportunity to exact a pound of flesh, if you will.

As differently as the American and British armies reacted to the enlistment of black soldiers, or the whole idea of arming blacks at all, so too were the circumstances different in the two opposing navies, only in the reverse. While many black men were running toward a British army, others ran toward the *American navy*. This is a fascinating contradiction. It's no secret that the life of a common British sailor was one of the most miserable experiences a man could endure. A sailor's lot was not only hard and the food pathetic, but the pay wasn't worth the danger. However, the new United States had no navy; owned no ships.

American sailors during the Revolutionary War were privateers sailing independently-owned vessels. Ships, such as the one captained by John Paul Jones, sailed under a Letter of Marque and were, therefore, treated by an enemy at sea as sailors in the service of their government and not as pirates. And like most privateers of that era, American sailors were paid equal shares of any booty, once the captain and Continental Congress received their cut. As a result, blacks in the American navy were equal to any seaman at their side and paid just as well, so long as they pulled their weight in their daily duties and in battle.

LETTERS OF MARQUE

A Letter of Marque was the difference between a legally appointed agent of king and country and a criminal—a privateer or a pirate—and these letters were honored by every European empire and nation. A Letter of Marque issued by a royal governor in the British colonies would have been respected by the captain of a French ship in the China Sea. In East Florida, Governor Tonyn issued many Letters of Marque, as the Royal Navy didn't see East Florida as being in harm's way during the Revolution and refused to provide a steady naval presence. Tonyn would build what he called a "fresh-water navy" from the local seamen who were willing to patrol the many rivers, creeks, and estuaries of northeast Florida.

Letter of Marque authorized by Benjamin Franklin showing the duration of the terms are from May 2, 1780 to March 27, 1781

Taking Control
of Their Own Destinies

I t should never be stated that the enslaved population of the American colonies didn't appreciate or take advantage of British assistance when it was offered, regardless of how insincere the offer might have been. But let's not forget how desperately Great Britain needed the slaves of rebellious colonists to be free—even if only for a short time (after all, they did plan on winning the war and then would need slaves to work their plantations!). The British used them to assist their armies, wreak havoc on the profits of rebel plantations, and to strike fear in the hearts of former owners at the thought of massive slave revolts. But that didn't mean that blacks in the American colonies were helpless.

In fact, history continues to expose the façade that enslaved Africans and African Americans were inferior in any way to those who held them in captivity. The American Revolution has been described by some as the largest slave revolt in American history, giving slaves the full understanding that they could actually influence their struggle by challenging the notion that blacks were less than human and had no rights to be treated as such. From these circumstances, many slave owners also began to take notice that times were changing, even if just slightly. Militias, led by southern planters such as Thomas Brown, fully understood the chaos created by the plundering of slaves and providing them with guns. Brown armed over 150 blacks—both free and enslaved—in the East Florida Rangers and believed that a more lenient slave code would make these men and those in other militias more reliable. Men like Brown knew that the best way to cripple another

The black militia of Fort Mose

Photo courtesy of Jackie Hird Photography

planter who had chosen the "wrong" side was to remove their slaves, and the best way to win the loyalty of those slaves was to treat them like men. Though it would be another nine decades before the end of slavery, the first cracks in the foundation would begin here; now. This is one of the legacies of the American Revolution that we rarely hear about, and it's long overdue.

As more Loyalists fled to East Florida, blacks here would meet their own spiritual needs. Johann D. Schoepf, a German traveler in East Florida at the end of the Revolution, "discovered a black Baptist minister preaching to a Negro congregation in a cabin outside of [St. Augustine]." It should be no surprise to see this kind of activity and in such a formalized setting as an established church. These were dark days and difficult times, and many of these people made unfathomable sacrifices to be in St. Augustine. For many, being in East Florida made their lives even more uncertain than before, making their spiritual needs great. Their minister was most likely an evacuee from one of the great early black Baptist churches at Silver Bluff, South Carolina, or in Savannah, where significant black Baptist churches were established in the mid-1770s.

But the important thing is that they met. They found their own clergy. They established their own church building. How fascinating it would be to learn of his sermon topics and his advice during these times. Though we have no records of the words he spoke, this activity was one of the loudest collective black voices in all of this study. For there, in that church, it can be assured that these people were expressing their views, sharing their sorrows, and comforting one another.

It's ridiculous to think that it took the British to spark the idea of escape so that blacks might fight against the very people who enslaved them. As long as there is a human spirit there is free will, and free will drives people to seek life; to seek liberty. Even today, those who are held captive for any reason, right or wrong, think of little else. The spirit of freedom lived in the minds of every slave, and revolt against their owners was often the only hopeful path to reclaiming their rights as free human beings. The British simply provided an opportunity for these people. Although the opportunity was quite often a false hope, one slight opening—just one lucky break—was all they hoped for.

Spirit of Freedom!

CONCLUSION

The interpreter, Gopher John, was one of the many "Black Seminoles" of his day

OR the many southern blacks who ended up in East Florida, that break wouldn't come until after the war. By January 1783, the population of the colony had swelled to nearly 22,000. Brigadier General Archibald McArthur calculated that three-fifths of that number—or approximately 12,500 people—were black. With such a large number filtering from across the South into one area, like East Florida, there is also a vast inconsistency in their circumstances once they had arrived. Some may have been free-born, perhaps due to their parents having been freed previously. Others found the same opportunity as Olauduah Equiano and purchased their own freedom, while still more were liberated by the recent British proclamations. There would be those who were still Loyalist slaves but had become separated from their owners on the journey south and had no idea what their status might be—they just knew to keep ahead of the American army. Still more were the slaves of Loyalist refugees from other colonies who were busily working on their owners' new plantations in East Florida. There were a good number of blacks who had been in East Florida for the entire war and must have wondered why some people were set free for taking up arms against the rebellion when they themselves had been doing that very thing for the past eight years.

But the human spirit is a wonderful thing. When the British completed their extended evacuation of East Florida on November 13, 1785, Governor Tonyn documented that 3,589 blacks were taken to the slave plantations of the Caribbean, while another 2,561 were sent back to former owners in the United States. 200 free blacks filed for Spanish citizenship, 155 left for Nova Scotia, and 35 departed for Deptford, England. But that only adds up to 6,540 people—approximately half the number estimated by General McArthur. Therefore, the question must be asked, what happened to the other 5,500–6,500 blacks who were never accounted for? We know that many took off for Seminole communities, and their descendants live in Florida and Oklahoma today. Others may have remained in the Floridas as free Spanish subjects, or perhaps they headed into what is now Texas or Mexico in search of opportunities west of the Mississippi River. Still others, who had the skills, took to the sea. But wherever they went, whatever they did, they were free. By their own determination, they were free.